W9-BMU-030

LEADERSHIP
SMARTS

Inspiration and Wisdom from the Heart of a Leader

Ken Blanchard

America's Best-Selling Business Author

Co-author *The One Minute Manager*®

HONOR BOOKS

Inspiration and Motivation for the Season of Life

COOK COMMUNICATIONS MINISTRIES
Colorado Springs, Colorado • Paris, Ontario
KINGSWAY COMMUNICATIONS LTD
Eastbourne, England

Honor Books® is an imprint of

Cook Communications Ministries, Colorado Springs, CO 80918

Cook Communications, Paris, Ontario

Kingsway Communications, Eastbourne, England

LEADERSHIP SMARTS—INSPIRATION AND WISDOM FROM THE
HEART OF A LEADER

Copyright © 2004 Blanchard Family Partnership

The Ken Blanchard Companies

125 State Place

Escondido, CA 92029-1398

First printing, 1998

Printed in Canada

3 4 5 6 7 Printing/Year 09 08 07 06 05

ISBN 1-56292-124-X

Introduction

When I was in high school, we had a football coach who loved motivational sayings. They covered the walls of our locker room. Sayings like, "When the going gets tough, the tough get going" and "Quitters never win and winners never quit" were imprinted in my mind. When I started teaching and writing in the field of leadership and management, it was second nature for me to use sayings to help people remember key points.

That's why I was thrilled when Honor Books asked me to write *The Heart of a Leader*, a book that included my favorite sayings. What you hold in your hands is an updated gift edition of that book, printed in an easy-to-carry format.

I hope these sayings will give you the leadership smarts you need to achieve high performance and remarkable results. I also hope you will come to realize that the best leaders are those who know their power flows through them, not from them.

God bless!

Ken Blanchard
June 2003

The key to
developing people is
to catch them doing
something right.

Ken Blanchard and Spencer Johnson
The One Minute Manager®

Catching people doing things right is a powerful management concept. Unfortunately, most leaders have a genius for catching people doing things wrong. I always recommend that leaders spend at least an hour a week wandering around their operation catching people doing things right.

People who produce
good results feel
good about
themselves.

Ken Blanchard and Robert Lorber
Putting the One Minute Manager® to Work

An effective leader will make it a priority to help his or her people produce good results in two ways:

1) Make sure people know what their goals are, and

2) Do everything possible to support, encourage, and coach them to accomplish those goals.

Praise progress.
It's a moving target.

Ken Blanchard, Thad Lacinak, Chuck Tompkins,
and Jim Ballard, *Whale Done!*™

When a good performance is followed by something positive, naturally people want to continue that behavior. It's important to emphasize here not to wait for *exactly* right behavior before you respond positively. Otherwise, you might wait forever.

Feedback is the breakfast of champions.

Rick Tate

I firmly believe that providing feedback is the most cost-effective strategy for improving performance and instilling satisfaction. It can be done quickly, it costs nothing, and it can turn people around fast.

When mistakes occur, redirect the energy.

Ken Blanchard, Thad Lacinak, Chuck Tompkins, and Jim Ballard, *Whale Done!*™

When people make a mistake they usually know it. What they really would like is advice on how they can avoid making the same mistake again. That's what redirection is all about— getting people's energy refocused on the right things.

No one can make
you feel inferior
without your
permission.

Eleanor Roosevelt

I go out into the world every day with the attitude that my "okayness" is not up for grabs. I firmly believe that "God did not make junk." This doesn't mean I don't have areas of my life that need improvement—just that at my basic core, I'm okay.

None of us is as smart as all of us.

Ken Blanchard, Don Carew,
and Eunice Parisi-Carew
The One Minute Manager®
Builds High Performing Teams

This quote has become the guiding principle of our team-building work in organizations. When I first caught the truth of this statement, it made me relax tremendously as a leader. I realized that I didn't have to be the only bright person in the group. In fact, admitting my vulnerability allowed me to ask for help. I'm convinced that any problem can be solved if we involve the resources we have gathered around us.

Things *not* worth
doing are not worth
doing well.

Ken Blanchard, William Oncken, and Hal Burrows
The One Minute Manager® Meets the Monkey

An effective leader must step back, look at the big picture, and make sure the important things are not pushed out of the way by the urgent needs of the moment.

If your people and customers are important, then you will spend part of every day making them feel that way. Evaluate each day by asking, "Have I done what is really important today?"

Success is not
forever and failure
isn't fatal.

Ken Blanchard and Don Shula
Everyone's a Coach

Don Shula had a twenty-four-hour rule. He allowed himself, his coaches, and his players a maximum of twenty-four hours after a football game to celebrate a victory or bemoan a defeat. During that time, they were encouraged to experience the thrill of victory or the agony of defeat as deeply as possible. Once the twenty-four-hour deadline had passed, they put it behind them and focused their energies on preparing for the next opponent.

Don't get a big head when you win or get too down in the dumps when you lose. Keep things in perspective. Success is not forever, and failure isn't fatal.

When you stop
learning, you stop
growing.

The only three things we can count on are death, taxes, and change. Since organizations are being bombarded with change, you would be wise to make learning a top priority and constantly strive to adapt to new circumstances.

In life,
what you resist,
persists.

Werner Erhard

If something is bothering you and you don't deal with it, you are gunnysacking your feelings— holding them inside. This can backfire later when you find yourself "dumping" in an inappropriate way and at exactly the wrong moment. It is also true that if you will deal with what is bothering you, the problem often disappears in the very process. Have you ever said, "I'm glad I got that off my mind"?

Don't work harder—
work smarter.

I f you don't take time out to think,
strategize, and prioritize, you will
work a whole lot harder, without
enjoying the benefits of a job smartly
done.

Nice guys may
appear to finish last,
but usually they are
running in a
different race.

Ken Blanchard and Norman Vincent Peale
The Power of Ethical Management

People today want what they want, and they want it right now. A negative side effect of such impatience is poor decision-making. Patience helps us to realize that if we do what is right—even if it costs us in the short run—it will pay off in the long run.

In managing people it is easier to loosen up than tighten up.

Ken Blanchard, Patricia Zigarmi, and Drea Zigarmi
Leadership and the One Minute Manager®

If you are not sure how much direction people need to do a task, it's always better to oversupervise than undersupervise in the beginning. Why? Because if you find your people are better than you thought, and you loosen up, they will like you and respond in a positive way.

It's easier to start off tough and then be nice than to start off nice and then get tough. It's easier to loosen up than tighten up.

Anything worth doing does not have to be done perfectly—at first.

It's counterproductive to be too hard on yourself. Don't expect instant perfection. While self-criticism is healthy, it should not be destructive. It's unfair to be hard on yourself the first time you attempt something new. It is also unfair to expect such an unrealistic standard from others. It's not necessary to do everything exactly right the first time.

What motivates
people is what
motivates people.

How do you know what motivation works with what employees? Ask! Try asking something like, "If you perform well, what reward or recognition could you receive that would make you want to continue to perform at a high level?" It pays to ask this important question.

Life is all about
getting A's.

During my ten years of college teaching, I sometimes got into trouble with other faculty members because I always gave out the final examination questions on the first day of class. When my colleagues asked why, I would reply, "Because I plan to spend the semester teaching them the answers, so when it comes time for the final, everyone will get an A."

After all, that's what life is all about!

Create Raving Fans®; satisfied customers are not good enough.

Ken Blanchard and Sheldon Bowles
Raving Fans®

Differentiate yourself from your competition by teaching your sales force and customer-service representatives—everyone who comes in contact with your public—to develop "raving fan" customers. Going the "extra mile" for the people who write your checks will pay off.

If you want to know why your people are not performing well, step up to the mirror and take a peek.

The main job of a leader is to help his or her people succeed in accomplishing their goals. When someone fails, good leaders accept responsibility for that failure. And when people accomplish their goals and win, everyone wins.

If you want your
people to be
responsible, you
must be responsive.

Ken Blanchard, Bill Hybels, and Phil Hodges
Leadership by the Book

People look to leaders for direction. But once goals are clear, your role as a leader changes. Your job becomes one of working *with* your people rather than having them work *for* you. Being responsive to your people's needs sets them free to be responsible (able to respond) for getting the job done.

It's more important
as a manager
to be respected than
to be popular.

Ken Blanchard and Don Shula
Everyone's a Coach

re you willing to push your people—whether it's a group of middle managers or a Cub Scout pack—beyond their comfort zone in order to achieve excellence? They might not like what you ask of them, but they will remember you as a leader they respected.

People with humility
don't think less of
themselves, they
just think of
themselves less.

Ken Blanchard and Norman Vincent Peale
The Power of Ethical Management

Agreat rule for doing business today is: Think more about your people, and they will think more of themselves. And don't act like you are perfect. Leaders need to come from behind their curtains of infallibility, power, and control, and let their "very good" side—their humanity—be revealed. Folks like to be around a person who is willing to admit his or her vulnerability, asks for ideas, and can let others be in the spotlight.

Never, never,
never, never . . .
give in.

Winston Churchill

Persistence means sticking to your guns. It's keeping your commitment and making your actions consistent with your word. It's all about "walking your talk."

Trying is just a noisy
way of not doing
something.

Many people are interested rather than committed. They talk about trying to do something, rather than actually doing it. They make lots of noise, but fail to follow up. An interested exerciser wakes up in the morning to rain and says, "I think I'll exercise tomorrow." A committed exerciser wakes up to rain and says, "I better exercise inside."

It never hurts to toot your own horn once in a while.

Ken Blanchard, Thad Lacinak, Chuck Tompkins,
and Jim Ballard, *Whale Done!*™

It's been said that if you don't toot your own horn, someone will come along and use it as a spittoon. As long as you're busy accentuating the positive with others, a little self-praise doesn't hurt. A lot of managers are hard on others because they're so hard on themselves. They're always after themselves in their heads; *Oh, I should have done that better,* or *What a dummy I am, forgetting that detail.* Sound like anybody you know?

Sometimes when the
numbers look right
the decision is still
wrong!

Ken Blanchard and Norman Vincent Peale
The Power of Ethical Management

Good business requires more than simply calculating which choice will make the most money. It requires developing some way to step back from things and put them in perspective. If you don't get things in perspective, you will continue to be driven only by the bottom line.

Love is being able to
say you're sorry.

My mother always said, "There are two statements that people don't use enough that could change the world: 'thank you' and 'I'm sorry.'" If as a leader you can give up being right and learn to apologize for your mistakes, your organization will be a lot better place for people to work. Thanks, Mom.

Without a change in your behavior, just saying "I'm sorry" is not enough.

Ken Blanchard and Margret McBride
The One Minute Apology

Saying "I'm sorry" is just the first step in an effective apology. The only way you can demonstrate that you are really sorry is by changing your behavior. That way the people you have harmed know that you are committed to not repeating the mistake. Talk is cheap—it's your behavior that matters.

Take what you do seriously but yourself lightly.

Ken Blanchard and Terry Waghorn
Mission Possible

Today's leaders must relearn the value of a smile or they will be unable to fire up the ability of their people to find real enjoyment in their work. So start thinking smiles until you become a smile millionaire. People will be glad to see you coming.

Perpetual prosperity comes to those who help others.

Ken Blanchard and Sheldon Bowles
Big Bucks!

Moneymaking is about what you can get. Perpetual prosperity is about what you can give. Success at the money level is about what you can achieve. Perpetual prosperity is about how you can serve. There are lots of good reasons to earn money, but some people seek money because of the power and status it will give them to control events and other people. When we reach out to help someone else, we often get more back in return. That's not why we help people; that's just how it works sometimes.

Think Big!
Act Big!
Be Big!

Norman Vincent Peale

Be your own best friend and believe in yourself. Don't wait for someone to do it for you. Cheer yourself on. Write your own pep talk. It works.

Real communication
happens when
people feel safe.

ind ways to convince your
people that you see them all
as either winners or potential
winners and you mean them no harm.
When you do, you will find that
communication within your
organization is greatly enhanced.

All good
performance starts
with clear goals.

An important way to motivate your people is to make sure they know where they are going. See that each person's goals are clearly defined and that he or she knows what good performance looks like. This will give them a clear focus for their energy and put them on the road to becoming high-performing, empowered producers.

Different strokes for different folks.

Ken Blanchard, Patricia Zigarmi, and Drea Zigarmi
Leadership and the One Minute Manager®

So what is the best leadership style? A "participative" style—listening to your people and involving them in decision making? Or a "directive" leadership style—until their knowledge and skills mature? The best leadership style is the one that matches the developmental needs of the person with whom you're working.

Different strokes for the same folks.

Ken Blanchard, Patricia Zigarmi, and Drea Zigarmi
Leadership and the One Minute Manager®

The point is that no individual is at any one stage in all the tasks he or she performs. Consequently, the same person may need different leadership styles (different strokes) for various tasks. For example, when I was a college professor, I loved to teach and write. Those were tasks I performed well and without supervision. However, when it came to administrative matters like managing my budget and filling out reports, I was a "Disillusioned Learner" at best. Sometimes it takes different strokes for the same folks.

If God had wanted
us to talk more than
listen, He would
have given us two
mouths rather than
two ears.

Ken Blanchard
We Are the Beloved

When you ask people about the best leader they ever had, one quality is always mentioned—they are good listeners. Test the power of listening for yourself by taking time to listen and focus on others.

Vision is knowing who are you, where you're going, and what will guide your journey.

Ken Blanchard and Jesse Stoner
Full Steam Ahead!

People need vision. During times of growth, change, opportunity, or uncertainty, a vision points us in the right direction. Collectively and individually, we need a significant purpose, clear values, and a picture that shows us what these look like when we are living them consistently. Vision gives meaning to our lives and provides direction. It helps us get focused, get energized, and get great results.

Vision is a lot more
than putting a
plaque on the wall.
A real vision is lived,
not framed.

Ken Blanchard and Jesse Stoner
Full Steam Ahead!

It's one thing to identify your vision. It's another to make it happen. You can't just go out and announce a vision and expect everyone to immediately understand it or agree to it. You have to be willing to allow others to help shape it. When a vision is shared, it is easier to hold each other accountable for behaving consistently with it. If you ignore the behavior of others who are not acting consistently with the vision, you threaten the trust and commitment of people who are. It takes courage to create a vision, and it takes courage to act on it.

If you don't seek
perfection, you can
never reach
excellence.

Ken Blanchard and Don Shula
Everyone's a Coach

The level of people's expectations has a great deal to do with the results they achieve. Don Shula's vision of perfection for the football team he coached was to win every game. Was that possible? No, but the 1972 Miami Dolphins did it for a season—establishing a level of perfection that no other NFL team has ever matched.

Don's philosophy is that if you're shooting at a target, you're better off aiming at the bull's-eye because if you miss it, the chances are high you'll still be on the target. On the other hand, if you aim just for the target and miss, you're nowhere.

Take responsibility
for making
relationships work.

Let me ask you a question—the same question you should be asking yourself, not only about your love relationship but also your relationship with your children, your boss, your co-workers, your direct reports, and your friends. *Do you want the relationship to work?* If so, then you must take personal responsibility for making it work. And forget the word "trying." Trying is just a noisier way of *not* doing something.

A river without banks is a large puddle.

Ken Blanchard, John P. Carlos, Alan Randolph
Empowerment Takes More Than a Minute

Don't send your people off on their own with no experience and then punish them when they make mistakes. Like the banks of a river, boundaries have the ability to channel energy in the right direction. Establish clear boundaries that will free them to make decisions, take initiative, act like owners, and stay on track.

Your game is only as good as your practice.

Ken Blanchard and Don Shula
Everyone's a Coach

No individual or team can reach "practice perfection" alone. It takes ferocious concentration and unyielding commitment to continuous improvement. That means day-to-day coaching—setting clear goals, letting people perform, observing, and then praising progress or redirecting efforts. "You can't coach from the press box," Don Shula used to say. "You have to be on the field."

All empowerment
exists in the present
moment.

onsider moments when you were at your best, and you will find that you were right there in the moment, fully and completely present. If you dwell only on "what was" or "what will be," you will miss the power of "what is."

We are not human beings having a spiritual experience. We are spiritual beings having a human experience.

Suppose that we accepted the fact that we have the unconditional love of God our Father—that we can't achieve enough, sell enough, build enough, or own enough to merit more love—we have all the love there is. Would knowing this truth make us better cheerleaders, supporters, and encouragers for our people? I think so. When you discover that you are a spiritual being having a human experience, you realize that everyone else is too.

You get from people
what you expect.

Whenever I talk about the power of catching people doing things right, I hear: "Yeah, right. You don't know Harry!" Do you have a "Harry" in your life? If so, perhaps you should take a look at your expectations for that person and see if he or she isn't currently living down to them.

I have never seen a
U-Haul® attached to
a hearse.

Rabbi Harold Kushner, author of *When Bad Things Happen to Good People*, said: "I've never heard someone on their deathbed say, 'I wish I'd gone to the office more!' They all say something like, 'I wish I'd cared more. I wish I'd loved more. I wish I'd reached out to others more.'"

The cure for too
much to do is
solitude and silence.

Ken Blanchard and Phil Hodges
The Servant Leader

Solitude and silence give us some space to reform our innermost attitudes toward people and events. They take the world off our shoulders for a time and interrupt our habit of constantly managing things, of being in control or thinking we are. In solitude and silence you find that you are more than what you do and that you are never truly alone.

People in
organizations need
to develop a
fascination for what
doesn't work.

few forward-thinking companies have learned to celebrate mistakes as opportunities for learning. I know of a large organization that shoots off a cannon when a big mistake is made. They're not saying they enjoy making errors; they're saying it's time for everyone to learn something. Other organizations would do well to adopt a similar policy. After all, how can they improve if they don't learn from their mistakes?

Winning coaches
make their teams
audible-ready.

Ken Blanchard and Don Shula
Everyone's a Coach

An "audible" is a football term—a verbal command used to alert the players to substitute new assignments for the ones they were prepared to perform.

I get frustrated with people who tell customers, "Sorry, that's our policy," even when the policy doesn't make sense. Teach your people to bring their brains to work and be audible-ready.

Never punish a learner.

Ken Blanchard and Spencer Johnson
The One Minute Manager®

When a learner makes a mistake, be sure that he or she knows immediately that the behavior was incorrect. Place the blame on yourself by saying, "Sorry, I didn't make it clear." Then patiently redirect by reviewing the assignment. If possible, demonstrate what a good job looks like. Observe the learner's new behavior in the hope of catching him or her doing something approximately right and praising progress.

People are okay, it's their behavior that's a problem sometimes.

Ken Blanchard and Spencer Johnson
The One Minute Manager®

People sometimes ask, "Why reaffirm someone you're upset with?" Reaffirming is important, because you want the person to walk away thinking about correcting the wrong behavior rather than how he or she has been mistreated or misunderstood. You want to get rid of the behavior rather than the person.

Consistency isn't behaving the same way all the time.

Ken Blanchard and Don Shula
Everyone's a Coach

Consistency does not mean behaving the same way all the time. It actually means behaving the same way under similar circumstances. I believe in praising people, but I also know that if you praise them when they are performing well and also when they are performing poorly, you are sending them an inconsistent message. Good performance should always be treated differently than poor performance.

When you respond to your people in the same way under similar circumstances, you give them a valuable gift—the gift of predictability.

This is the first time
in the history of
business that you
can be great at what
you're doing today
and be out of
business tomorrow.

Ken Blanchard and Terry Waghorn
Mission Possible

Constant change is a way of life in business today. In fact, to stay competitive, you must simultaneously manage the present and plan the future.

The problem is, you can't have the same people doing both jobs. If people with present-time operational responsibilities are asked to think about the future, they will kill it. If people with responsibilities for the future also have present-time duties, the urgent problems of today will drag them away from tomorrow's opportunities.

The only job
security you have
today is your
commitment to
continuous personal
improvement.

You must make up your mind to control your circumstances by means of continuous personal improvement. The sign on your bathroom mirror should say, "Getting better all the time."

When you know
what you stand for,
you can turn around
on a dime and have
five cents change.

Ask yourself how long it would take your people to process a major product change, get behind it, and still meet deadlines. The key to an outstanding, enthusiastic, flexible, and on-time team is to make sure your people are values-driven, rather than goals-driven. If the number one shared value is to serve the customer, then they will be ready to do whatever it takes to live that value.

Share the cash, then share the congratulations.

Ken Blanchard and Sheldon Bowles
Gung Ho!®

You can pat your people on the back and congratulate them all you want, but if you're not taking care of their need for cash, these praisings won't ring true.

A large segment of our U.S. population is hurting financially. So remember, if you want to build credibility, the rule is: first cash, then congratulations.

There is no pillow
as soft as a clear
conscience.

John Wooden

The number one characteristic employees say they are looking for in a leader is integrity. Meeting people with a clear conscience puts you at ease and allows you to concentrate on doing your best work. When you deal straight with people, they sense that they can trust you. And when you lie down at night, your clear conscience makes a wonderfully soft pillow.

It's surprising how much you can accomplish if you don't care who gets the credit.

Abraham Lincoln

Sharing credit is all about self-esteem. People who have to get all the credit and act like they are the only ones who count are actually covering up their own "I-don't-count" feelings.

Suppose tomorrow you are struck by a lightning bolt that increases your self-esteem by 100 percent. Would you act differently? Sure you would. Would you be willing to share credit with your people? Of course. Would they perform better as a result? You had better believe it. Let's hope for some lightning bolts!

Positive thinkers
get positive results
because they are not
afraid of problems.

Ken Blanchard and Norman Vincent Peale
The Power of Ethical Management

People often asked Norman Vincent Peale, "Don't you think life would be better if we had fewer problems?" Norman would answer that question by saying, "I'll be happy to take you to Woodlawn Cemetery because the only people I know who don't have any problems are dead."

In fact, if you really insisted that you had no problems, he would suggest that you immediately race home, go straight to your bedroom and slam the door, then get down on your knees and pray: "What's the matter, Lord? Don't You trust me anymore? Give me some problems!"

Early in life, people give up their health to gain wealth. . . . In later life, people give up some of their wealth to regain health!

Ken Blanchard, D. W. Edington, and Marjorie Blanchard
The One Minute Manager®
Balances Life and Work

If you don't watch out, success can kill you. When *The One Minute Manager®* leaped onto the best-seller list, I found myself running around the country giving speeches, conducting interviews on radio and TV—doing all the things that seem to come with material success.

One day I looked at myself and realized I was overweight, not exercising, sleep deprived, and generally treating my body like it was indestructible. My wife, Margie, was telling me I needed to get my life in balance. I had to give up some of my wealth to regain my health. What are you doing?

Am I a servant leader or a self-serving leader?

Ken Blanchard and Phil Hodges
The Servant Leader

One of the quickest ways you can tell the difference between a servant leader and a self-serving leader is how he or she handles feedback, because one of the biggest fears that self-serving leaders have is to lose their position. Self-serving leaders spend most of their time protecting their status. If you give them feedback, how do they usually respond? Negatively. They think your feedback means that you don't want their leadership anymore. Servant leaders embrace and welcome feedback as a source of useful information on how they can provide better service.

Ducks quack.
Eagles soar.

I once tried to rent a car in Ithaca, New York. I had planned to fly out of Syracuse, so I asked for a car from Syracuse in order to avoid the drop-off fee. The clerk located a car from Syracuse, but the $50 fee remained on my contract. "I can't take it off; my computer won't let me and my boss would kill me," she quacked. It took me twenty minutes to get this woman to remove the drop-off fee. Eagles flourish in organizations where the customer is the focus, while ducks multiply in places where boss-pleasing and policy-following carry the day.

Eagles flourish when they're free to fly.

I was greeted the minute I walked into the DMV to replace my lost driver's license. "Welcome. Do you speak English or Spanish?" a woman asked. She then ushered me to a counter where a smiling young man asked how he could help me. Nine minutes later, I had a temporary license.

I walked over to meet "the boss" and found him to be a servant leader. He told me that it was his job "to reorganize the department on a moment-by-moment basis, depending on customer needs." His commitment to take care of citizens was obvious.

Duck-busting was that manager's way of life. He wanted eagles who would create *Raving Fan*® customers. I certainly went away from there as one.

Get your ego out of the way and move on.

Ken Blanchard, Sheldon Bowles,
Don Carew, and Eunice Parisi-Carew
High Five!

The minute you decide to be part of a team, you're going to lose some things and gain some things. What you're going to gain is synergy—one plus one equals more than two. What you're going to lose is getting your ideas automatically accepted. If you're going to be part of a winning team, you have to be willing to accept some losses. Fight for your ideas certainly. Try to convince others. But if they can't or won't buy into your thinking, it's time to take a deep breath and let go.

New today,
obsolete tomorrow.

Things are happening so quickly today that it's almost impossible to be a "know it all" anymore. These days, within a year, most managers know far less than their people about what they do. Not admitting this can lead to real problems.

One of the most ingratiating things you can do with your people is to admit your ignorance or vulnerability. Once done, this opens the door for others to share their expertise, and for you to become a cheerleader, supporter, and encourager.

So if you're obsolete, who cares? Someone around you will have the answer, and your ignorance will allow him or her to shine.

G.O.L.F. stands for Game of Life First.

Ken Blanchard
The One Minute Golfer
(formerly *Playing the Great Game of Golf*)

I've often said I can find out more about someone during one round of golf than by working with them for a long period of time. Golf brings out the best and worst in people. If you cheat or blow up when you have a bad break, that same behavior will show up in other parts of your life. If you maintain a positive attitude when things go sour, that will carry over into other things also. What better training ground is there than the golf course for learning to accept the bitter with the sweet? Go ahead! Tee it up!

Leadership is not something you do *to* people. It's something you do *with* people.

Ken Blanchard, Patricia Zigarmi, and Drea Zigarmi
Leadership and The One Minute Manager®

When you share your leadership strategy with your people, they not only understand what you have in mind but they can give you helpful feedback. True servant leaders want feedback because they are anxious to know whether their interactions with their people are helpful and effective. So don't do leadership *to* people, do it *with* them.

Don't settle for less than a Fortun*ate* 500 company.

Ken Blanchard and Michael O'Connor
Managing by Values®

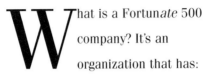

What is a Fortun*ate* 500 company? It's an organization that has:

1) Motivated customers who keep coming back;

2) Inspired employees who give their best each day;

3) Owners who enjoy profits made in an ethically fair manner;

4) Significant others (suppliers, community, vendors, distributors, and even respected competitors) who thrive on the mutual trust and respect they feel toward the company.

Take time to
identify core values.

Identifying the core values that define your organization is one of the most important functions of leadership. The success or failure of this process can literally make or break an organization.

You would be wise to make the identification of your organization's core values a top priority. And don't try to do this job alone. Take advantage of the resources you have around you. Draw in your people—everyone should have ownership in this process. Remember that rules can be imposed but values cannot. Bring everyone into the process early.

Core values must be communicated.

I dentifying your organization's core values is a worthless exercise unless those values are constantly communicated and your people and customers see that you are completely committed to them.

In fact, it's impossible to affirm them too much. Talk about your organization's values; put them on your business cards, annual reports, plaques, wall signs, and job aids. In short, display them anywhere your people, customers, stockholders, and significant others can see them.

Walk your talk.

Without some method of locating gaps between values and behavior, identifying and communicating core values will do more harm than good. An organization that talks about putting the customer first, for example, but fails to do so, is far more likely to be judged harshly by its people and customers alike.

This means that it is vital for organizations and their leadership to "walk their talk." They must make every effort to become living symbols of their organization's value system.

Knowing where
you're going is the
first step to getting
there.

Ken Blanchard
We Are the Beloved

Have you identified your mission in life—your reason for being? Establishing a personal mission statement is an important exercise that has helped me define who I am, identify my priorities, and keep my perspective on target. It involves identifying your passions.

Let God help you find the driving force in your life. Doing so is the first step to a happier and more satisfied you.

As a leader, the
most important
earthly relationship
you can cultivate is
your relationship
with yourself.

Ken Blanchard and Terry Waghorn
Mission Possible

Do you really know yourself? Do you have a personal mission statement that defines your strengths and motivates you to be all God meant you to be?

You might want to try an interesting activity that will almost certainly help you develop a clearer sense of purpose and personal identity: Write your own obituary.

I know it sounds strange—even a little morbid. But this exercise is not about dying; it's about living. It will give you an opportunity to adjust your life, describe the ideal you, and define what it is you would like to be remembered for. Why leave such important matters to chance? God has a wonderful plan for your life. Let Him help you establish your path and guide you as you walk in it.

Purpose can never
be about
achievement; it is
much bigger.

Ken Blanchard and Terry Waghorn
Mission Possible

The beauty of writing your own obituary before you die is that it serves as a dream—a big picture of what you want your life to be and mean. So, if you don't like the way your life is shaping up right now, change it. Don't hold back! God made you, and He has always intended for you to be the best that you can be. He not only approves, but I have found that He is willing and able to help in your search for self-discovery. Quiet yourself, pray, and listen to the voice that says, "You are loved, richly and unconditionally."

Purpose has to do
with one's calling—
deciding what
business you are in
as a person.

Ken Blanchard and Norman Vincent Peale
The Power of Ethical Management

I once heard a story about Alfred Nobel, the originator of the Nobel peace prize. When his brother died, Nobel got a copy of the newspaper to see what was said about his brother. He was shocked to discover that a dreadful error had been made. The paper had confused him with his brother and the obituary he was reading was his own.

As a young man, Alfred Nobel had been involved in the invention of dynamite, and his premature obituary elaborated on the terrible death and destruction this powerful force had brought into the world. Nobel was devastated. He wanted to be known as a man of "peace." He quickly realized that if his obituary was to be rewritten, he would have to do it himself by changing the nature of his life. So he did just that. I dare say that Alfred Nobel is better known today for his contribution to peace rather than for any other thing he did in his life.

Your life is yours to design. Make it all it can be!

About the Author

Millions have looked to Ken Blanchard to help improve their leadership skills. He is the Chief Spiritual Officer of The Ken Blanchard Companies, a company that he and his wife, Dr. Marjorie Blanchard, founded in 1979. Ken co-authored *The One Minute Manager*® with Spencer Johnson, and the book has sold more than 13 million copies in 25 languages. A captivating and much sought-after speaker, he is cofounder of the Center for FaithWalk Leadership.

About The Ken Blanchard Companies

The Ken Blanchard Companies is a global leader in workplace learning, employee productivity, and leadership effectiveness. Building upon the principles of Ken's books, the company is recognized as a thought leader in leveraging leadership skills and recognizing the value of people to accomplish strategic objectives. Through seminars and in-depth consulting in the areas of teamwork, customer service, leadership, performance management, and organizational change, The Ken Blanchard Companies not only helps people learn but also ensures they cross the bridge from learning to doing.

If you enjoyed this book, a short videotape that creatively captures these philosophies is available. Please contact:

The Ken Blanchard Companies
125 State Place
Escondido, CA 92029
800/728-6000 or 760/489-5005
www.kenblanchard.com

Other Titles
by Ken Blanchard

The One Minute Manager®
with Spencer Johnson, 1981

Leadership and The
One Minute Manager®
with Patricia Zigarmi and Drea Zigarmi,
1985

The Power of Ethical Management
with Norman Vincent Peale, 1988

The One Minute Manager®
Meets the Monkey
with William Oncken and Hal Burrows,
1989

The One Minute Manager® *Builds High*
Performing Teams
with Don Carew and Eunice Parisi-Carew,
1990

Raving Fans®
with Sheldon Bowles, 1993

Everyone's a Coach
with Don Shula, 1995

Empowerment Takes
More Than a Minute
with John Carlos and Alan Randolph, 1996

Gung Ho!®
with Sheldon Bowles, 1998

Leadership by the Book
with Bill Hybels and Phil Hodges, 1999

High Five!
with Sheldon Bowles, Don Carew, and Eunice
Parisi-Carew, 2001

Whale Done!™
with Thad Lacinak, Chuck Tompkins, and Jim
Ballard, 2002

The Generosity Factor
with S. Truett Cathy, 2002

The Servant Leader
with Phil Hodges, 2003

The One Minute Apology™
with Margret McBride, 2003

Full Steam Ahead!
with Jesse Stoner, 2003

The Leadership Pill
with Marc Muchnick, 2003

Additional copies of this and other
Honor Books products are available wherever
good books are sold.

If you have enjoyed this book,
or if it has had an impact on your life,
we would like to hear from you.

Please contact us at:

HONOR BOOKS
Cook Communications Ministries, Dept. 201
4050 Lee Vance View
Colorado Springs, CO 80918
Or visit our Web site:
www.cookministries.com

Inspiration and Motivation for the Season of Life